Night of the Living Poems

Virginia Marshall

BookLeaf
Publishing

Presentation by *BookLeaf Publishing*

Web: www.bookleafpub.com

E-mail: info@bookleafpub.com

ISBN: 978-93-5873-795-0

First edition 2023

DEDICATION

I want to dedicate this book to all of my family and friends. My best friends Mary, Tammy, Jamie, and Karley, you are like sisters to me, and I appreciate you all so much. My aunts Cynthia, Maria, and Lisa, thank you for always being there for me and instilling great values in my life. My uncles, Jerry and Howie, thank you for teaching me how to drive and for my first legal beer. My Mom and Dad, thank you for having me and allowing me to go nuts with Halloween stuff as a kid. My brother, you were always my rock and I miss you dearly. My nephew Dylan and my niece Victoria, I love the two of you so much and wish everything had been so different. You both deserved better!

ACKNOWLEDGEMENT

I'd like to thank Jamie Andrews for letting me know about this writer's challenge. I have known her since my childhood, and she is an amazing person as well as an excellent friend.

PREFACE

They're coming to get you!

Forehead Kisses

A kiss on the lips can be loveless and fleeting

But a kiss on the forehead, now that's intriguing

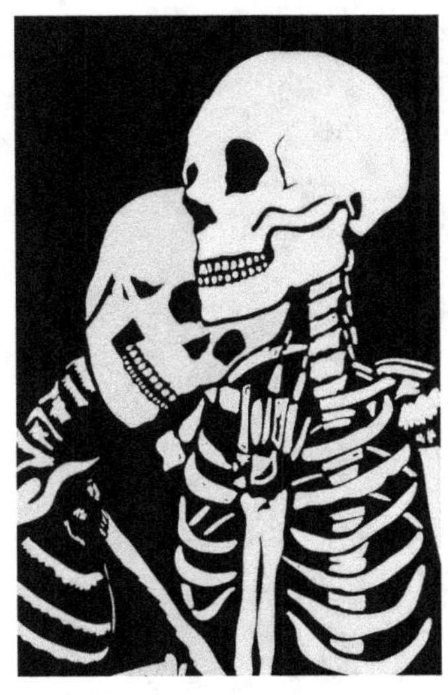

HER

Her eyes look so innocent
Hiding her deceit

Her touch is so soft
Burning right through me

Her arms held so tightly
I could not breathe

Her smile was so charming
As sinister as could be

Her words are so comforting
As lies often are

Her lips were so inviting
Leaving nothing but scars

Love Bombing

I should have known better and have myself to blame

When we first met, she was with another, but on a dating site, I saw her name

A week later, and she's now single, so I said okay

On our first date, she told me things that would make most people run away, but I told myself that people could change

Six months later, I'm in love but feeling mentally drained

I tell her this isn't working, and she says she will change

She says she doesn't have a place to call home, so she makes my home her own

After a year of all her love bombing, I started to see her crack, so I suggested she try on different hats

I'm not perfect by any means, but I have been supportive, honest, loving, and loyal, yet she continues putting me down and threatens to leave

I look in the mirror and no longer see me

I have become a shell of the person I used to be

She wrecks her car, and I bend over backward to help her

Still, I'm feeling less and less at ease

On my 40th birthday, her love bombing returned, and I told myself I could make this work

I brought her iced coffee to her job, and something felt off

That night, I called her crying, and she laughed at me

I already knew what was coming next, and I had no more fight in me, so I just agreed

Ten days go by of being set free, and then I log in to find out she was cheating on me

Night Terror

5

Breathe

Slow and steady
You start trembling

Breathe

Soaked in sweat
You start screaming

Breathe

Startled awake
You start reaching

Breathe

Searching in the dark
You start seeing

Breathe

Sounds of weeping
You start hearing

Breathe Breathe Breathe

She's outside underneath the willow tree,
haunting you with memories

Nobody Is Perfect

Every day, she complained about my faults,
while every day I embraced hers

Longing For A Love That Was Never Real

Holding her always felt wrong
Like there was nothing there all along

Kissing her was never deep
It's like my body knew she didn't love me

Talking to her, I was always scared
Like walking on eggshells

In all my times of need
She was nowhere to be seen

So why do I miss her like I do
I haven't got a clue

Quietly Into The Night

I did not go quietly into the night as some
thought I might

Instead I stood my ground and put up a fight

She went around telling lies about me, so I told
the truth about her

The price I paid took its toll

For those that matter already know, it was those
who do not I was trying to show

Now, I must find a way to let this all go

Bad Apple

Looks so tasty

Fits perfectly in my hand

I close my eyes

Take a bite

Now I'm choking

Will they all be bad

Garden State

Her reality was not reality at all

I tried to bring her back, but she was too far
gone

Maybe it was I who was in the wrong for
wanting her to come back to a reality where she
did not feel she belonged

As I tried and tried to stay strong the more
games she played so, of course, I followed right
along

She's a beautiful hot mess that tried to destroy
me

Her doctor gave her meds that turned her into a
zombie

The next day, she was gone, so I sat and stared

I started to notice all but one of her rabbit holes
had disappeared

I make a promise to myself not to go down it
this time, for I'm afraid I may lose my mind

I place her favorite rock over the hole and walk
away

I hope she knows how much I truly loved her
and still do today

Two Face

Your personality was fake, but the pain it caused was very real

Holding Me Under

Screaming underwater

No one sees or hears

Was it even real

She holds me under

Fighting for air as she smiles

All I can do is wonder

As I find comfort in the icy cold water

12-Foot Skeleton

I can buy myself a 12-foot skeleton

Write my name in quicksand

Talk to black cats for hours

Cast spells you can't comprehend

I can take myself Halloween shopping

And hold a ghost's hand

Yes, the spooky season loves me better than you can

Rotten To The Core

You can be the most beautiful person in the world, but that beauty is worthless when you are rotten to the core

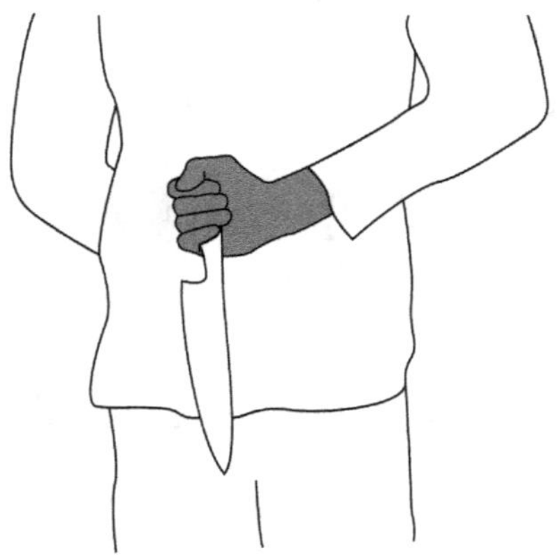

The Twilight Zone

She tried to make me think I was going crazy
while the whole time she was cheating on me

Do you think I would get an apology

No, but she shows up at my house unexpectedly

She asked me to call her mistress to tell her what
a stand-up person she is after all the years of
abusing me

Have I lost my mind? Nope, this is reality

I never did get that apology, but now it would
mean absolutely nothing

Pathological Liar

Oh, the lies keep coming

But now I just laugh

You and I both know this new relationship of
yours won't last

Keep on lying to yourself, but you really need
some professional help

Did you ever tell her the whole truth

I didn't think so

The Mask

Eventually, her mask will fall off

And you will finally see

We are all just pawns in her little schemes

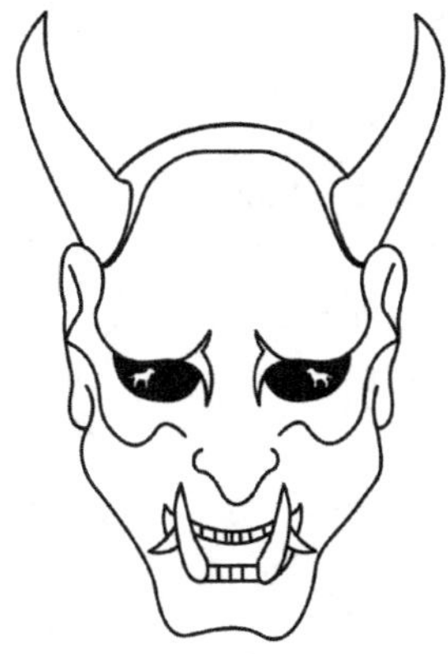

Skeletons

Did you hear that

Your closet door just broke

Looks like that sage didn't work

Your skeletons are now out, and karma is on her way

Better grab those crystals

You have a considerable debt to pay

Grief

Someone once said grief is love with no place to go

So I grab my pen and let it flow

With hopes that all this love turned to hate will dissipate

Last Dance

Call me crazy, but I enjoy honesty

Without it, there's no you and me

Once it's gone, that's the end of our song

Letting Go

There's a full moon in the sky

So bright that it blinds

Like the light you use to see in my eyes

It's not there any longer

We both know why

You took me for a ride

Now it's time I say goodbye

Fall

Autumn leaves are falling as pumpkin spice
lattes are brewing

You can smell the burning of bonfires in the
crisp October air

As the days get shorter and the nights get longer,
there's no other place I'd rather be than in your
arms, on our couch, in our oversized hoodies